HAMILTON EAST PUBLIC LIBRARY

W9-AAS-240

FISHERS

We Love Holidays

Celebrating Id-Ul-Adha: A Muslim Festival

Alice Green

j 297.36 Gre 2009
Green, Alice.
  Celebrating Id-Ul-Adha
  2008030374   1/10
  1435829050

INV 1-10

PowerKiDS press.

New York

Hamilton East Public Library
One Library Plaza
Noblesville, IN 46060

Published in 2009 by The Rosen Publishing Group Inc.
29 East 21st Street, New York, NY 10010

Copyright © 2009 Wayland/The Rosen Publishing Group, Inc.

All rights reserved. No part of this book may be reproduced in any
form without permission from the publisher, except by a reviewer.

First Edition

Series Editor: Jean Coppendale
Senior Design Manager: Simmi Sikka
Designer: Diksha Khatri

Library of Congress Cataloging-in-Publication Data

Green, Alice.
  Celebrating Id-ul-Adha : a Muslim festival / Alice Green. – 1st ed.
      p. cm. – (We love holidays)
  Includes index.
  ISBN 978-1-4358-2845-2 (library binding)
  ISBN 978-1-4358-2905-3 (paperback)
  ISBN 978-1-4358-2909-1 (6-pack)
  1. 'Id al-Adha--Juvenile literature. 2. Islam–Rituals–Juvenile literature. I. Title.
  BP186.6.G74 2009
  297.3'6–dc22
                                2008030374

Manufactured in China

The publishers would like to thank the following for allowing us to reproduce
their pictures in this book:
Corbis: title page, 20, Studio DL; 13, Christine Osborne; 9, Kazuyoshi Nomachi /
Alamy: 4, 23, Charles O. Cecil / Ali Abbas: 5 / Photolibrary: 6, Photo Researchers,
Inc. / REUTERS: 7, Aladin Abdel Naby; 8, Crack Palinggi; 11, Ali Jarekji; 15,
Bazuki Muhammad; 21, Ajay Verma / EPA: 10 / THE HINDU: cover, 12, 19, 22,
14, / Alexander Boden: 16 / Islamic Relief: 17 / wildphotos.com: 18, Anil Dev.

Contents

Web Sites
Due to the changing nature of Internet links, PowerKids Press has developed an online list of Web sites related to the subject of this book. This site is updated regularly. Please use this link to access this list: www.powerkidslinks.com/wlh/adha

Families get up early on eid morning to bathe and prepare for their visit to the mosque. Special prayers are said in the mosque. After prayers people visit their friends and relatives to wish them happy eid.

Happy Id!

Children and men from Oman, in the Middle East, wearing traditional clothes on a picnic during Id-ul-Adha.

Id-ul-Adha is one of the most important Muslim festivals. It is celebrated two months after Id-ul-Fitr, a festival which comes at the end of **Ramadan**, the month when Muslims **fast** through each day.

Id-ul-Adha also marks the end of **Hajj**. This is a journey, or pilgrimage, that Muslims make to their holy city of Makkah, or Mecca, in Saudi Arabia.

Hajj pilgrims visit the masjid-al-Haram mosque in Makkah.

DID YOU KNOW?

Id-ul-Adha is also known as Hari Raya Aidiladha in Indonesia and Malaysia. In Turkey, Muslims call it Kurban Bayrami.

A story of sacrifice

Boys read the Holy Qur'an, or Koran, on Id-ul-Adha. The Qur'an contains the story of Ibrahim ﷺ and Ishmail.

Ibrahim ﷺ is one of the **prophets** of Islam. Muslims believe that Allah (the Muslim name for God) appeared to Ibrahim ﷺ in a dream and asked him to **sacrifice** his son, Ishmail, to show his obedience to Allah. Ibrahim ﷺ followed Allah's orders and took Ishmail to Mina, a city near Makkah.

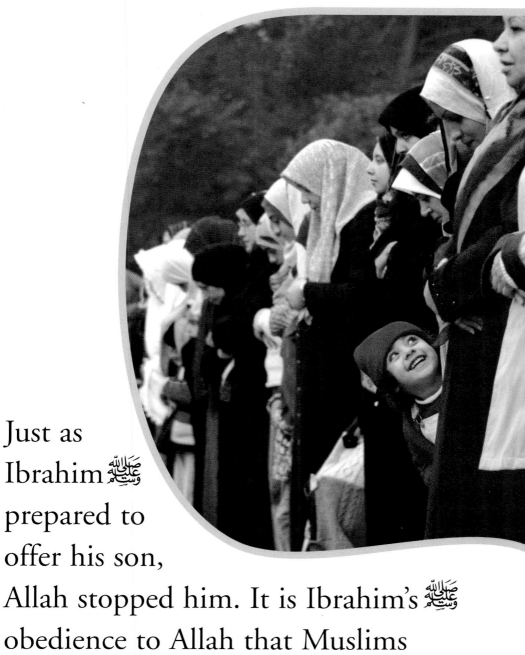

Women in Cairo, Egypt, pray during Id-ul-Adha. Men and women pray in separate places; some women pray in their homes.

Just as Ibrahim ﷺ prepared to offer his son, Allah stopped him. It is Ibrahim's ﷺ obedience to Allah that Muslims celebrate every year at Id-ul-Adha.

Sacred pilgrimage

The festival of Id-ul-Adha takes place on the last day of Hajj. During Hajj, Muslims travel the same path that Ibrahim ﷺ took to Mina to sacrifice Ishmail.

These Indonesian pilgrims are flying to Makkah for the Hajj.

Millions of
Muslims arrive
at Makkah
about nine days
before Id-ul-Adha.
When they get there,
they have to do certain things. These
include walking around the **Ka'bah**,
a large square-shaped building in the
middle of the Sacred Mosque in Makkah.

The Ka'bah, in the center of this picture, is the holiest building for Muslims. They believe that it was built by Ibrahim ﷺ and Ishmail.

DID YOU KNOW?

**Muslims always face the direction
of the Ka'bah when they pray.**

End of the pilgrimage

Throughout Hajj, Muslim men wear special white clothes. This is so they all look the same before Allah.

On the tenth and final day of Hajj, Muslims gather at Mina for their last duty. The pilgrims begin the day by throwing pebbles at the Jamarah, a stone pillar that stands for the devil.

The devil tried to persuade Ibrahim ﷺ not to do as Allah asked. The devil tried to **tempt** Ibrahim ﷺ and Ishmail three times. Each time they drove him away by throwing seven stones at him.

Muslims gather at the Jamarah pillar to throw their stones.

DID YOU KNOW?

Muslims believe that the Jamarah pillar stands on the spot where the devil appeared before Ibrahim ﷺ.

Visit to a mosque

Muslims offering Id-ul-Adha prayers at Moti Masjid, in Bhopal, India.

On the day of Id-ul-Adha, Muslims around the world who are not on Hajj wake up early and put on new clothes. Then they gather at a mosque to join in morning prayers.

Id-ul-Adha is a time when Muslims ask Allah to forgive their sins, and to help them become kinder and stronger.

A mu'adhin, from a mosque in Cairo, Egypt, calls Muslims to prayer.

Exchanging greetings

After prayers, Muslims hug and greet each other. Then they visit family and friends, and celebrate the festival of Id-ul-Adha together.

Two boys in Patna, India, greet each other on Id-ul-Adha.

Many Muslims also take time to visit **cemeteries** and pray for their family and friends who have died.

A Malaysian boy pours rose water on his mother's grave on Id-ul-Adha.

Feast of Sacrifice

Id-ul-Adha teaches the importance of looking after each other and obeying Allah. Many Muslims buy meat from special stores and give some of it to the poor.

Muslims in London, U.K., buy meat from stores such as this one on Id-ul-Adha.

JUST QUALITY HALAL MEAT   FRESH WHOLESALE & RETAIL

0207 733 5556   0798 4164067

Food being
distributed
to the poor
during
Id-ul-Adha
in California.

Muslims make sure that no one is
hungry on this special day. The pilgrims
in Makkah also hand out food and
money among poor pilgrims.

Delicious feast

Muslims make delicious food as a part of the Id-ul-Adha celebrations. Different kinds of food are made by Muslims around the world.

A boy enjoys a bowl of sweets prepared specially on Id-ul-Adha.

Biryani, a dish made with rice and lamb, is a favorite with lots of children in India. Many Indonesian Muslims make rice cakes that are eaten with lamb or chicken curry.

A feast of biriyani and kebabs.

DID YOU KNOW?

The Muslims of Oman, in the Middle East, make a special sweet dish called halwa. It is made of wheat, sugar, and almonds.

19

children's delight

Part of Id-ul-Adha is also a children's festival. Many children receive presents from their family and friends.

A Malaysian mother gives her son money on Id-ul-Adha.

Many Muslim parents take their children out on picnics or to amusement parks. The children spend the day having fun.

An Indian father buys balloons for his son.

DID YOU KNOW?

Some Muslims living in Rehaniya, Israel, give coins to all the children in the village on this day.

21

Colorful celebrations

Some Muslims spend Id-ul-Adha outdoors. Many go shopping for candy and presents for their friends and relatives.

People in Srinagar, India, shop for Id-ul-Adha gifts.

In some countries, such as Jordan and the United Arab Emirates, music and dance are an important part of the celebrations.

Children watch men perform a special dance as a part of the Id-ul-Adha celebrations in Al-Hamra, Oman.

Index and further information

GLOSSARY

cemeteries special places where the dead are buried

fast to go without food or beverages

Hajj the yearly pilgrimage, or journey, to Makkah (Mecca), which all Muslims try to make at least once in their lives

Ka'bah a black, square-shaped structure built in the middle of the Great Mosque at Makkah

mu'adhin the person who calls Muslims to prayer from a mosque

prophets religious leaders who are thought to be messengers of God

Qur'an the holy book of Islam. Also called the Koran

Ramadan the month in the Islamic year when Muslims fast between sunrise and sunset

sacrifice to kill a person, or animal, as an offering to a god

tempt to try to make someone do something wrong by promising a reward in return

BOOKS TO READ

Ramadhan and Id-ul-Fitr by Azra Jessa (Tahrike Tarsile Qur'an, 2008)

Religions of the World: Islam by David Self (World Almanac Library, 2006)

This is My Faith: Islam by Anita Ganeri (Barrons Educational, 2006)